Italian complete cousine Cookbook

Comprehensive Italian Meals And Recipes

By

William A. Davis

The trademarks that are used are without any consent, and the publication of the trademark is without permission or backing by the trademark owner. All trademarks and brands within this book are for clarifying purposes only and are the owned by the owners themselves, not affiliated with this document.

Table of contents

Introduction

Italy has a vast array of culinary masterpieces. such a broad palette of colors, which are different in every single geographic area, and within each geographic area, differing by individual territory, and in each individual city. It is truly the destina- tion of the new Grand Tour, which now not only seeks beauty in archaeology, architecture, art, or landscapes, but also in time-honored delicacies with a modern heart. Here, history, climate, envi- ronment, manual dexterity, and culinary genius have merged, and continue to blend into an inimi- table harmony.

Artichoke salad with Parmigiano-reggiano cheese; Penne All'Arrabbiata; Branzino All'Acqua Pazza; mixed fish fry; capon stuffed with chest- nuts; asparagus with Parmigiano-reggiano cheese; Baci di dama with cacao; peaches with amaretti; zabaglione. This is a mere glimpse of a possible gastronomic itinerary along the Italian peninsula, and the list goes on. It is estimated that in Italy there are over 3000 typical dishes, just counting

the fundamental ones. There are many more, if we take into account the numerous creative variants that each recipe has carried along with itself over time. For this volume, the Academia Barilla has selected 100 easy recipes from Italian cuisine, all characterized by the same straightforward execu- tion. While being quite aware of having left out many others, we have collected those considered the best — for quality, truth, and wisdom — for rais- ing awareness of the primacy of Italian cuisine. In these recipes, respect for the territory — seen not only as a physical space, but also social and cul- tural — and investment into the legacy of the past have come together, with a pinch of poetry and innovation.

not only the typical dishes have been conse- crated by tradition, but also the creations that are typically Italian for their successful alchemy of gastronomic intuition, executive ability, and use of great products typical of the Bel Paese. examples include buffalo mozzarella from Campania, Pecori-

THe eleGAnCe oF sImPlICITy

no romano, radicchio di Treviso, Taggiasca olives, balsamic vinegar of modena, sicilian pistachios, and Piedmontese hazelnuts. And in the culinary uni- verse of the peninsula, even though there are dish- es with considerable complexity, the overwhelm- ing majority are characterized by the elegance of simplicity: They require just a few ingredients of very high quality, and the creativity and care to bring out their best in just a few steps. Perhaps this is because the majority of the jewels of Italian cuisine—which also include many recipes of aristo-cratic ancestry—come from dishes with a humble origin, and were born making use of inexpensive, everyday ingredients, yet filled with imagination and flavor. For example, classic Vermicelli with To- mato sauce has exquisite originality because of its very simplicity. such recipes have turned necessity into a virtue. These are simple preparations, but were quickly admitted into the most esteemed din- ing halls, and have now risen to the ranks of refined specialties.

some of them can boast service for centuries, if not millennia. Just think of the traditional cream of fava beans. even the ancient romans had a pas- sion for this legume, as proven by their many rec- ipes still used on the peninsula today. other dish- es are more recent, yet have already entered into the olympus of the most representative recipes of Italy. The gourmet Tiramisu, for example, one of the most well-known spoon desserts, was born in a restaurant in Treviso, in the Veneto region, in the late 1960s.

The fame of Italian cuisine, however, depends not only upon the delicacy of the dishes them- selves, prepared with skill and with quality prod- ucts, but also upon the way it expresses the sig- nificance of a good life. The food is a metaphor for a lifestyle that is typically Italian: sunny, open, creative, and joyful, where good humor gives you an appetite, and vice versa. And this philosophy — an outlook on the kitchen, but also on the world — is something that all Italians have in common.

Salads & Vegetables

The vegeTable garden on your plaTe

There is no other gastronomy in the world that holds vegetables so dearly as Italian cuisine. It is a sin- cere love, with its roots going back into the mists of time, owing to the precious heritage of agricultural cultivation that the Bel Paese can boast from north to south: from the red radicchio di Treviso to Pachino cherry tomatoes, from the green asparagus of Romag- na to Roman artichokes, from Tropea onions to the eggplants of Sicily. And the love for this green wealth has been further reinforced in recent years, because many people have become interested in a vegetarian diet,whether for reasons related to health, ethics, or the environment. Not only has the Bel Paese's gastro- nomic culture always made use of produce from the garden to prepare the various dishes that make up a meal, but it has even succeeded in making them the stars of side dishes. Here, they are enjoyed raw or cooked by various methods, whether steamed, stewed, sautéed, baked au gratin, marinated, fried, sautéed "truffle-style," or grilled, and served on their own or

combined with other ingredients. As a side dish, vege- tables accompany a main course dish of meat or fish, but may also be considered lighter, flavorsome main courses in and of themselves.

This is particularly so if they are reinforced by protein ingredients, like baked potatoes filled with fresh goat cheese, or or fennel au gratin, flavored with butter and a generous sprinkling of Parmigiano-Reggiano.

Naturally, if a side dish is served as a side, it should be presented in a reduced quantity, so as to maintain a certain harmony of pro- portions with the main dish it accompanies. If instead, it is to assume the dignity of a main course, the quantity can be increased. These vegetable-based recipes, so typically Italian, are not only a fantasy of colors, textures, and fragrances, but a treasure trove of taste, and should be prepared using seasonal ingredients. They should also be correctly matched with the dishes they are to accompany, selected for their affinity or contrast, but never for homogeneity, so as to "escort" the main dish, to its side or in front of it.

4 Servings

1 3/4 lbs. (800 g)

asparagus

1/2 stick (60 g) unsalted

butter

2 oz. (50 g) grated Parmigiano-Reggiano, or about 1/2 cup

salt

parMa STyle aSparaguS

preparation: 15 minutes

Cooking: 10 minutes

bring a pot of well-salted water to a boil.

Trim the hard ends from the asparagus and cut all of the stalks the same length. Tie the asparagus in small bundles with butcher's twine and boil, with the tips pointing upward to avoid damage, until tender but still firm, about 10 minutes. drain, remove the twine, and arrange the asparagus on a serving dish.

Sprinkle the asparagus tips with the parmigiano-reggiano.

In a small saucepan, melt the butter and cook until frothy. pour it over the aspara- gus and serve.

4 Servings

1 lb. (500 g) eggplant, diced

7 oz. (200 g) red onion, diced 14 oz. (400 g) red bell

peppers, diced

10 1/2 oz. (300 g) ripe tomatoes, diced

3 1/2 oz. (100 g) black olives

3 1/2 oz. (100 g) raisins, or about 2/3 cup packed

1 oz. (30 g) pine nuts, or about 3 1/2 tbsp., toasted

bunch fennel, diced

1/3 cup (80 ml) red wine vinegar

1/3 cup (80 ml) extra-virgin olive oil

cloves garlic

1/2 oz. (15 g) fresh basil, or about 30 leaves

salt and pepper

eggplanT Salad WITh Fennel, olIveS, and raISInS

Clean and dice each vegetable separately. In a small bowl of warm water, soak the raisins for 15 minutes; then drain them and squeeze out any excess liquid.

heat the oil in a pan over medium heat and sauté the onion. add the eggplant, peppers, fennel and garlic and let cook until the eggplant softens, about 10 minutes. add the olives and raisins, and then add the tomatoes. Stir in the basil, and season salt and pepper.

Cover the pan and let the liquid reduce for 5 minutes, stirring occasionally. remove the cover, add the sugar and vinegar, and let the vegetables continue to cook until the mixture is dense and the vegetables are tender. garnish with basil and pine nuts and serve.

preparation: 30 minutes

Cooking: 20 minutes

JeWISh STyle arTIChoKeS

4 Servings

1 1/2 lbs. (600 g) globe artichokes 3 1/2 oz. (100 g) lemon, juiced extra-virgin olive oil, as needed salt and pepper

preparation: 20 minutes

Cooking: 25 minutes

remove the hard outer leaves of the artichokes, and trim the stem, leaving about 1 inch (3 cm).

With a very sharp knife, trim all around the head of each artichoke to remove the hard part of the leaves. In a bowl, combine the lemon juice with water and put the cut artichokes in the water so they don't turn brown.

Clip a deep fat/candy thermometer to the side of a large skillet. add enough of the oil so the artichokes will be immersed when added to the pan. heat the oil to about 270°F (130°C).

drain and dry the artichokes. Knock them against each other and then flatten them lightly on a chopping board by pressing on the base so the leaves spread out. Sprinkle a pinch of salt and pepper inside the leaves that are no longer tightly closed.

Fry the artichokes in the oil until you can easily insert a knife in the flesh, about 20 minutes. Transfer to paper towels to drain. Just before serving, heat the oil to 340°-350°F (170-180°C) and fry the artichokes again until crunchy, 3-5 minutes. drain on paper towels and serve hot.

4 Servings

3 1/3 lbs (1.5 kg) broccoli rabe, trimmed and chopped into large pieces

10 tsp. (50 ml) extra-virgin olive oil

2 cloves garlic, thinly sliced

chili peppers to taste

salt

STIr-FrIed broCColI rabe

preparation: 15 minutes

Cooking: 10 minutes

heat the extra-virgin olive oil in a skillet with the finely sliced garlic and the chili pepper, and cook until the garlic is golden; do not let the garlic brown too much. add the broccoli rabe, season with salt, and cook over medium heat, stirring frequently, 10 minutes. Serve.

4 Servings

14 oz. (400 g) fennel bulbs

3.5 oz. (100 g)

Parmigiano-Reggiano, grated, or about 1 cup

3 1/2 tbsp. (50 g) unsalted butter

salt

baKed Fennel WITh parMIgIano-reggIano

heat the oven to 375°F (190°C).

bring a pot of well-salted water to a boil. Cook the fennel in the boiling water un- til crisp-tender, then drain. let cool and cut into thick slices.

grease a baking dish with some of the butter, then melt the remaining butter in a small saucepan. In the baking dish, arrange a layer of fennel. Sprinkle with part of the grated parmigiano-reggiano and a bit of the melted butter. add a second layer of fennel and continue in the same manner until you have used all of the in- gredients.

bake the fenel until browned, crust, for about 10 minutes. Serve immediately.

preparation: 10 minutes

Cooking: 20 minutes

4 Servings

1 lb. (500 g) porcini mushrooms

5 tsp. (25 ml) extra-virgin olive oil

1 clove garlic

1 tbsp. fresh parsley, chopped

salt and pepper

preparation: 20 minutes

Cooking: 5-6 minutes

FrIed MuShrooMS WITh garlIC and parSley

Trim the mushrooms and clean them thoroughly, removing the soil and wiping them with a damp cloth. Slice them about 1/12 inch (2mm) thick.

heat the olive oil in a skillet and sauté the chopped garlic until fragrant; do not burn it. add the mushrooms and the parsley and cook until the mushrooms are tender. Season to taste with salt and pepper and serve.

4-6 Servings

1 1/3 lbs. (600 g) yellow, white, and purple potatoes, boiled with the skins on

1/3 cup plus 1 1/2 tbsp. (100 ml) plain yogurt 1/3 cup plus 1 1/2 tbsp. (100 ml) extra-virgin

olive oil

Fresh chives, for garnish

salt

poTaTo Salad

peel the potatoes, cut them into 1-inch cubes, and put them in a serving bowl. In another bowl, mix the yogurt with the extra-virgin olive oil and a pinch of salt.

dress the potatoes with the sauce. arrange the salad on a serving plate, decorat- ing it with strands of fresh chives, and serve.

preparation: 20 minutes

vegeTarIan STaCKS

4 Servings

preparation: 30 minutes
Cooking: 15 minutes

10 oz. (300 g) ripe tomatoes

7 oz. (200 g) yellow bell peppers

5 oz. (150 g) grated celeriac

7 oz. (200 g) summer squash

5 oz. (150 g) radicchio

7 oz. (200 g) fennel

9 oz. (250 g) zucchini

6 small eggplants

7 oz. (200 g) red onions

7 oz. (200 g) leeks, white parts only generous 1/3 cup (100 ml) milk

3 tbsp. (50 ml) extra-virgin olive oil All-purpose flour

Vegetable oil for frying

salt and pepper

Cut the white parts of the leeks into thin strips. Soak for 10 minutes in the milk, then drain. Coat in flour. bring a skillet of oil to a boil and deep-fry the leeks. drain on a paper towel, season with salt, and set aside. roast or grill the peppers, peppers in the oven or grill them, then peel them and slice them into rounds. Slice the eggplant, onion, and zucchini into rounds of about 1/8-inch (3 mm) thick. Slice the celeriac and squash, then, using a pastry cutter, slice them into discs the same size as the other vegetables. Slice the tomatoes, fennel, and radicchio.

put a few drops of water into a pot of salted boiling water, and cook the celeriac for 5 minutes. In another pan of boiling water, parboil the pumpkin for one minute. heat the oven to 475°F (245°C). drizzle the eggplant, onion, zucchini, celeriac, squash, fennel, and radicchio with olive oil and roast in a roasting pan for about 35 minutes. (grilling the vegetables is an option). place all the cooked vegetables in a bowl, season with salt and pepper and a drizzle of oil and let marinate for at least 15 minutes. layer vegetables to create stacks. garnish with the deep-fried leeks and serve.

4 Servings

7 oz. (200 g) arugula

5 oz. (150 g) Parmigiano- Reggiano

3 1/2 tbsp. (50 ml) extra- virgin olive oil

1 tbsp. (15 ml) balsamic vinegar

salt and pepper

preparation: 15 minutes

arugula Salad WITh parMIgIano-reggIano

In a small bowl, whisk together the balsamic vinegar, salt, pepper, and oil. Thinly shave the parmigiano-reggiano with a vegetable peeler.

arrange the arugula on individual plates and sprinkle with the cheese. drizzle with the dressing and serve.

4 Servings

1 3/4 lbs. (800 g) potatoes

5 oz. (150 g) fresh goat cheese

salt and pepper

poTaToeS STuFFed WITh goaT CheeSe

heat the oven to 350°F(180°C). Wrap them potatoes individually, skin on, in alu- minum foil. and bake for about 30 minutes. When cool enough to handle, cut them open. Season with a pinch of salt, top each with some of the fresh goat cheese and a sprinkle of pepper, and serve.

preparation: 10 minutes

Cooking: 30 minutes

Desserts

A finAle... in sweetness

Little delights of pastry crust, held together by an elegant veil of chocolate. Delicate and voluptuous waves of cream you could dive into. Inviting geomet- ric forms of sweetness to could get lost in. Cakes with crispy centers of dried fruits and treasure chests of puff pastry with unexpectedly fragrant fillings. Re- freshing and colorful scoops of ice cream and soft sorbet. Fruit scrumptiously covered with chocolate, or lavishly filled with sweetness.

Just think how much creativity would be gone from cooking if we did not have desserts. The Italian cuisine, in particular, would be bereft of large part of its glorious tradition.

All of the regions of the Bel Paese, in fact, have the good fortune of a rich legacy of traditional sweets, from the simplest, most ordinary, and easy to make to the most elaborate, spectacular, and time- consuming: the small pastry and many fried delights and spoon desserts, the bewitching cakes, the classic donuts, and the rustic tarts. Then there are the ever- so-Italian family of ice creams, sorbets, and soft ice creams, and the lighter preparations made from fresh fruits.

There are also the "specialty" desserts, usually on- ly available locally in limited areas, which nearly al- ways emerged as ritual symbols linked with sacred events. At one time limited to religious festivals or pri- vate events, these now can be commonly found in pas- try shops and private homes in their territory of ori- gin.

Other recipes, while representing local or region- al pride, are so well known and widespread along the peninsula that they have become national delicacies. There is Apple Strudel, representing Alto Adige; the delicious Cannoli, a veritable masterpiece of Sicil- ian pastry making; the Baci di Dama cookies with cacao and Zabaglione, Piedmontese delicacies; the Sbrisolona cake, a star dessert from Mantua; the Can- tucci with almonds, traditionally to be dipped in Vin Santo, the glory of Prato and Tuscany; and the delec- table Tiramisu, with its origins in the Veneto region.

Dessert is becoming increasingly important in the Italian meal. Not as a necessity, but it certainly is pleasant. Perhaps also for its almost therapeutic na- ture, and not simply for its gourmet attraction. A dessert doesn't merely delight the palate; it warms and cuddles the soul.

lADY's Kisses

4 Servings

Preparation: 40 minutes

Resting: 30 minutes

Cooking: 15 minutes

1 cup (125 g) all-purpose flour 1/2 cup plus 2 tbsp. (125 g) sugar 3/4 cup (100 g) roasted hazelnuts

scant 1/4 cup (25 g) blanched almonds

generous 1/2 cup (125 g) unsalted butter, softened 1/4 cup plus 2 tbsp. (30 g) cocoa powder

3 1/2 oz. (100 g) dark chocolate, roughly chopped

in a blender, pulse the hazelnuts and almonds with the sugar until finely ground. transfer the mixture to a bowl and mix with the butter.

sift the flour and cocoa powder together, then incorporate into the nut mixture, stirring as little as possible. wrap the mixture in plastic wrap and refrigerate for at least 30 minutes.

Heat the oven to 325°f (160°C).

Using a rolling pin, roll out the mixture on a lightly floured pastry board to a thickness of about 3/8 inch (1 cm). Cut out discs with pastry rings 5/8 to 3/4 inch (1.5 to 2 cm) in diameter and shape into balls with your hands.

Butter and flour a baking sheet or line it with parchment paper. Arrange the balls on the baking sheet and bake for about 15 minutes. let cool completely, then remove the balls from the pan and turn them upside-down.

Meanwhile, melt the chocolate in a heatproof bowl that fits snugly over a pot of barely simmering water (or in the microwave). let the chocolate cool and when it starts to thicken, pour a little on each of half of baci di dama. Gently press the remaining baci di dama on top of the chocolate and let set.

CReAM PUffs

4 Servings

Preparation: 25 minutes

Cooking: 20 minutes

fOR tHe PUffs

generous 1/4 cup plus 2 tbsp. (100 ml)
water

3 1/2 tbsp. (50 g) unsalted butter, cut into pieces

1/2 cup (60 g) all-purpose flour

2 large eggs salt

fOR tHe CReAM fillinG 4 cups (500 ml) milk 3/4 cup (150 g)
sugar

4 large egg yolks

generous 1/8 cup (20 g) all-purpose flour, sifted

2 1/2 tbsp. (20 g) cornstarch, sifted 1/2 vanilla bean, split

Bring the water to a boil in a pan with the butter and a pinch of salt. sift the flour, and when the water is boiling, add it all at once, then stir with a whisk. when the mixture begins to thicken, switch to a wooden spoon and continue to cook over medium heat until the mixture no longer sticks to the sides of the pan, 2 to 3 min- utes. Remove from the heat, let cool slightly, then stir in the eggs one at a time, on- ly adding the second egg when the first one has been completely incorporated.

Heat the oven to 375°f (190°C) and butter a baking sheet. fill a pastry bag fitted with a 1/4 in (6-7 mm) smooth tip. Pipe the cream puff mixture onto the baking sheet and bake for about 20 minutes.

Meanwhile, prepare the filling. Bring the milk to the boil in a pan with the vanilla bean. in a bowl, beat the egg yolks with the sugar with a whisk.

incorporate the cornstarch and flour. Pour about a quarter of the boiling milk mix- ture into the egg yolk mixture and stir until the mixture is perfectly combined. then pour this mixture into the rest of the milk and return to the heat. Return to a boil and continue to cook, whisking constantly. Pour the cooked cream filling in- to a bowl and let it cool it quickly.

to assemble the cream puffs, put the filling in a pastry bag fitted with a tip. Cut the top off each cream puff and fill with the cream. serve.

siCiliAn CAnnOli

4 Servings

Preparation: 28 minutes

Resting: 30 minutes

Cooking: 2 minutes

fOR tHe DOUGH

3/4 cup plus 1 tbsp. (100 g) pastry flour

2 tbsp. (10 g) unsweetened cocoa

3 1/2 tsp. (15 g) sugar

1 large egg

1 tbsp. marsala wine or rum 1 tbsp. (10 g) unsalted butter

1 pinch salt

fOR tHe fillinG

9 oz. (250 g) fresh ricotta (preferably made from sheep's milk)

1/2 cup (100 g) sugar

1 oz. (25 g) candied fruit, roughly

chopped

1 oz. (25 g) dark chocolate, roughly chopped

oz. (25 g) pistachio nuts, roughly chopped

olive oil for frying, as needed

confectioners' sugar, for decorating

Combine the flour, cocoa, butter, egg, sugar, and a pinch of salt on a work surface; then add the marsala and continue to knead. when the dough is homogeneous, let it rest for about 30 minutes.

Meanwhile, prepare the filling: Pass the ricotta through a sieve into a bowl, stir in the other filling ingredients, and refrigerate.

Roll out the dough and cut it into 4-inch (10 cm) squares. wrap the squares diag- onally around metal cannoli tubes.

Pour enough oil into a Dutch oven or other heavy pot so that it will be deep enough to submerge the cannoli. Heat the oil, and when hot, fry the cannoli for 1-2 minutes. As soon as the dough becomes golden, remove from the oil, drain on paper towels, and let cool. then remove them from the metal tubes.

spoon the cannoli filling into a pastry bag and fill the cannoli. Dust with confec- tioners' sugar and serve immediately. (After some time, the humidity of the filling will make the dough lose its crispness.)

VAnillA AnD CHOCOlAte iCe CReAM

Ingredients for approximately 2 pints (900 ml) of ice cream

fOR tHe CHOCOlAte

Preparation: 20 minutes

2 1/8 cups (500 ml) milk

2/3 cup (130 g) sugar

oz. (50 g) unsweetened cocoa, or about 1/2 cup

1/2 oz. (15 g) dextrose, or about 6 tsp. 1/8 oz. (3.5 g) stabilizer, or about 1 tsp. 1/3 oz. (10 g) dark chocolate, chopped

Maturation: 6 hours

Prepare an ice bath by filling a large bowl with several inches of ice water. set a smaller metal bowl in the ice water.

Heat the milk to 115°f (45°C); check with an instant read thermometer. in a bowl, combine the sugar, dextrose, and stabilizer, and pour the mixture into the milk in a steady stream. Heat the milk mixture to 150°f (65°C) and continue to cook until it reaches 185°f (85°C). stir in the chocolate. transfer the mixture to the bowl in the ice bath and cool rapidly. Refrigerate at 40°f (4°C) for six hours and then freeze the mixture in an ice cream maker according to the manufacturer's instructions.

fOR tHe VAnillA

2 cups plus 2 tbsp. (500 ml) milk

3 large egg yolks

3/4 cup (150 g) sugar

1/2 oz. (20 g) dextrose, or about 8 tsp.

2 cups plus 2 tsp. (15 g) powdered skim milk

1/8 oz. (3.5 g) stabilizer, or about 1 tsp.

5 tbsp. (50 g) heavy cream

1 vanilla bean, split

Heat the milk with the cracked vanilla bean to 115° f (45°C); check with an instant read thermometer and then remove the vanilla bean. Mix the sugar, powdered milk, dextrose and stabilizer and pour the dry mixture in a steady stream into the milk. Heat to 150°f (65°C), add the cream, and continue to cook until it reaches 185°f (85°C). Cool rapidly by putting the mixture in a container and immersing it in an ice water bath. Refrigerate at 40°f (4°C) for six hours and then freeze the mixture in an ice cream maker according to the manufacturer's instructions.

8 Servings

2 cups (250 g) all-purpose flour

3/4 cup plus 2 tbsp. (175 g) sugar

4 1/2 oz. (125 g) almonds 1/2 tsp. (2 g) baking soda 2 (95 g) large eggs

2 (30 g) large egg yolks

1 pinch (1 g) salt

pure vanilla extract, to taste

AlMOnD COOKies

Preparation: 20 minutes

Cooking: 20 minutes

Heat the oven to 350°f (180°C) line a baking sheet with parchment.

Mix all the ingredients together and knead them together until the dough is smooth and homogeneous. form the dough into logs and arrange them on the baking sheet. Bake for about 20 minutes. while the logs are still hot, cut them into into diagonal slices. Return them to the oven and bake until golden on both sides.

4 Servings

1 1/2 lbs. (700 g) apples, such as Reinette or Golden Delicious

3 oz. (80 g) apricot preserves, or about 1/4 cup

1 1/2 oz. (40 g) raisins, or about 1/4 cup packed

1/2 oz. (40 g) slivered almonds, or about 1/3 cup

tbsp. (25 g) brown sugar

BAKeD APPles witH RAisins AnD AlMOnDs

Heat the oven to 325°f (160°C).

Make a circular incision around each apple with the tip of a knife so it doesn't burst in the oven. Remove the core with an apple corer.

in a bowl, stir together the raisins and preserves and fill each apple with the mix- ture. sprinkle the brown sugar on top.

Arrange the apples in a baking dish, sprinkle the almonds over the tops, and bake for about 15 minutes.

Preparation: 20 minutes

Cooking: 30 minutes

133

MilK CHOCOlAte MOUsse

6 Servings

Preparation: 45 minutes

Cooling: 3 hours

Cooking: 50 minutes

fOR tHe MOUsse 1 cup (250 ml) milk 2 large egg yolks

9 oz. (250 g) milk chocolate, chopped 7 oz. (200 g) semi-whipped cream

1/3 oz. (10 g) gelatin sheets

fOR tHe BAtteR 1/2 cup (100 g) sugar 3 large eggs

1 large egg yolk

2/3 cup (80 g) all-purpose flour

2 1/2 tbsp. (20 g) potato starch or cornstarch

3 tbsp. (15 g) unsweetened cocoa pow- der

fOR tHe sYRUP 2 tbsp. (30 ml) water 3/8 cup (80 g) sugar

2 1/2 tbsp. (35 ml) rum (or other liqueur)

Heat the oven to 450°f (230°C). line a baking sheet with parchment.

to make the dough for the chocolate layer, sift together the flour, starch, and cocoa. separate the eggs and whisk the egg whites in a bowl with the sugar. in another bowl, stir the egg yolks with a fork. fold in the egg whites, then add the flour mixture. trans- fer to the baking sheet and spread so that the mixture is about 3/8 inch (1 cm) thick. Bake for 5 to 7 minutes.

to make the syrup, bring the water and sugar to a boil in a saucepan. Boil until the sug- ar is dissolved and remove from the heat. when cooled, stir in the rum and set aside. to make the mousse, put the chopped chocolate in a bowl. soften the gelatin in a bowl of cold water. Add the egg yolks and the milk and cook over low heat to pas- teurize the mixture, stirring constantly, until it reaches 185°f (85°C); check with an in- stant read thermometer. Remove from heat. squeeze the gelatin, and add it to the mixture so that it melts. immediately pour the mixture onto the chopped chocolate and stir thoroughly to obtain a smooth, even texture. let cool to 86°f (30°C).

whip the cream, which must stay fairly soft, then gently fold it into the chocolate mix- ture with a spatula.

to assemble, line the bottom and sides of a springform pan with the dough and drench it with syrup. fill with mousse, smooth it with a spatula, and refrigerate for at least 3 hours. Remove from the mold and decorate as desired.

Cover the top with chocolate curls if desired.

CHOCOlAte BUll's-eYes

Ingredients for 12 cookies

Preparation: 1 hour

Resting: 1 hour

Cooking: 13-15 minutes

fOR tHe CHOCOlAte sHORtBReAD 1 1/4 cups (165 g) all-purpose flour 1/4 cup plus 2 tbsp. (95 g) unsalted

butter, softened

generous 1/4 cup plus 2 tbsp. (85 g) sugar

2 large egg yolks

1/4 tsp. (1 g) baking powder

7 tsp. (9 g) unsweetened cocoa powder

Pinch vanilla powder salt

fOR tHe fillinG
2 tbsp. (30 g) orange marmalade

fOR tHe GAnACHe

2 oz. (60 g) dark chocolate, chopped 4 tbsp. (60 ml) heavy cream

1 tsp. (6 ml) glucose syrup

sift the flour and baking powder onto a piece of parchment. in a bowl, mix the butter with the sugar, stirring in a pinch of salt and the egg yolks. Add flour sift- ed with baking powder, the vanilla powder, and cocoa powder, and then knead briefly until you have a smooth dough.

wrap the dough in plastic wrap and refrigerate for at least 1 hour.

Heat the oven to 350°f (180°C) and grease and flour (or line with parchment) two baking sheets. On a lightly floured work surface, roll out the dough until just un- der 1/4 inch (4-5 mm) thick. Using a pastry ring with a 2-inch (5 cm) diameter, cut out discs (you'll need two discs for each finished bull's-eye).

Divide the dough discs equally between the baking sheets. Using a pastry ring with a 1 1/2 inch (4 cm) diameter, make a hole in the center of each disc on the first pan so that you have rings. transfer the pans to the oven and bake for 12 to 13 minutes, removing pan with rings a couple of minutes earlier than the one with discs. let cool completely.

turn the discs over and spread them with orange marmalade. top with the rings (the marmalade will ensure that they adhere).

to make the ganache, put the chocolate in a bowl. in a small saucepan, bring the cream to a boil with the glucose syrup. Pour the hot mixture over the chocolate. let cool slightly, put the ganache in a pastry bag fitted with a tip, and fill the cavity of the bull's-eyes.

CHOCOlAte-COVeReD AlMOnDs AnD HAZelnUts

4 Servings

Preparation: 40 minutes

1 1/2 tbsp. (20 g) sugar

2 tsp. (10 ml) water

1 cup (125 g) almonds and hazelnuts

1 tsp. (5 g) unsalted butter

6 oz. (180 g) dark chocolate, melted

Put the sugar and water in a saucepan and bring to a boil.

Add the almonds and hazelnuts, then cook until the sugar is amber in color. stir in the butter, then pour the mixture onto a baking sheet to cool, separating the almonds and hazelnuts.

Once the nuts have cooled, put them in a large bowl and add about a quarter of the chocolate.

stir so that the chocolate does not solidify, keeping the almonds and hazelnuts well separated.

Repeat until you have finished adding all of the chocolate. transfer the chocolate- coated nuts to a large-mesh sieve set over a bowl, and let the excess chocolate drain off. transfer the nuts to parchment and let them set. store in a dry place at room temperature, preferably in sealed glass jars or in cans with a lid.

4 Servings

fOR tHe MeRinGUe 1/4 cup plus 2 1/2 tbsp. (80 g) sugar

2 tbsp. plus 2 tsp. (40 g) large egg whites

1 tbsp. plus 1 tsp. (20 ml) water

fOR tHe MOUsse 2/3 cup plus 1 tbsp. (170 ml) heavy cream

1/4 cup plus 2 tsp. (70 ml) lemon juice

1/3 oz. (10 g) gelatin sheets

1 tbsp. plus 1 tsp. (20 ml) extra-virgin olive oil

Preparation: 30 minutes

freezing: 2 hours

leMOn MOUsse witH eXtRA-ViRGin OliVe Oil

to make the meringue, add the water and 1/3 cup of the sugar to a small saucepan and bring to a boil. Meanwhile, in a stand mixer or using an electric hand mixer, beat the egg whites with the remaining sugar in a bowl. (Alternatively, you can use a whisk.) when the sugar water reach 250°f (121°C) — check with an instant read thermometer — slowly add it to the egg whites and keep beating until it cools.

soak the gelatin in cold water for 5 minutes, then slowly dissolve it in a saucepan over low heat or in the microwave. whip the heavy cream and fold it into the meringue along with the gelatin and lemon juice.

Pour the mixture into individual molds and freeze them until set, about 2 hours. Unmold the mousse onto serving plates and drizzle with extra-virgin olive oil before serving.

4 Servings

1/2 cup (125 ml) milk

1/2 cup (125 ml) heavy cream

3 1/2 tbsp. (50 g) sugar

1 sheet (1/5 oz.) gelatin

PAnnA COttA

in a saucepan, bring the milk, cream and sugar to a boil.

Meanwhile, soak the gelatin in a bowl of cold water. squeeze it out, and add the gelatin to the milk mixture. stir well, taking care to avoid froth forming, and then pour the mixture into individual molds. Refrigerate for several hours.

Unmold the panna cotta and serve. try garnishing with a chocolate or caramel sauce, or with a fruit sauce made with strawberries, kiwis, or pears. Alternatively, sprinkle with chopped hazelnuts or pistachios.

Preparation: 20 minutes

Resting: 3 hours

4 Servings

1 lb. (500 g) peaches

5 amaretti cookies, crushed

3 tbsp. plus 2 tsp. (20 g)

unsweetened cocoa

2 large eggs

1/4 cup plus 1 1/2 tbsp. (70 g) sugar

Preparation: 20 minutes

Cooking: 30 minutes

PeACHes stUffeD witH AMARetti COOKies

Heat the oven to 325°f (160°C) and line a baking sheet with parchment.

Halve the peaches, remove the pits, and use a spoon to scoop out a bit more flesh from the center. Chop it up and mix it with the 2 egg yolks, amaretti and cocoa. in a bowl with an electric mixer, beat the egg whites with the sugar until stiff peaks form. fold them into the amaretti mixture.

Arrange the peach halves on the prepared baking sheet. fill with the amaretti mixture and bake for about 30 minutes. serve warm or cold.

4 Servings

fOR tHe Peels
4 1/2 oz. (130 g) candied orange peel, quartered

fOR tHe GlAZe 2 1/2 oz. (70 g) dark
chocolate

CHOCOlAte-COVeReD ORAnGe Peels

Arrange the candied orange peel quarters on a wire rack and let dry at room tem- perature overnight. the next day, cut them into strips about 1/4 inch (5-6 mm) wide and temper the dark chocolate: Melt the chocolate in a bain marie or microwave at 113–122°f (45–50°C) (use a cooking thermometer). Pour one-third to one-half onto a marble surface. let this cool until it reaches 79–81°f (26–27°C), then add it on top of the remaining hot chocolate. when the temperature of this new mixture reaches 86–88°f (30–31°C), it is ready to be used. Glaze the candied orange peels in the tem- pered chocolate using a fork. Drain the excess chocolate and place the chocolate- covered orange peels on a sheet of parchment. let set at room temperature.

Preparation: 12 hours

4 Servings

1 1/4 cups (300 g) confectioners' cream (see recipe below)

7 cups (415 g) unsweetened whipped cream

About 1/2 cup (135 g) Italian style meringue (see recipe below)

3 oz. (80 g) hazelnut paste

fOR tHe CReAM 2 large egg yolks

6 tbsp. (75 g) sugar

2 tbsp. (28 g) all-purpose flour

1 cup (250 ml) milk

fOR tHe MeRinGUe 2 large egg whites

1/2 cup plus 1 tbsp. (120 g) sugar

4 tsp. (20 ml) water

Preparation: 1 hour

freezing: 3 hours

PieDMOnt HAZelnUt seMifReDDO

to prepare the italian style meringue, clip a thermometer to the side of a small saucepan and heat two-thirds of the sugar and the water. Meanwhile, whisk the egg whites in a bowl with the remaining sugar until stiff. when the sugar mixture in the saucepan reaches 250°f (120°C) — check with an instant read thermometer — pour it onto the whipped egg whites and continue to whisk until lukewarm. set aside.

to make the confectioner's cream, beat the egg yolks in a bowl with the sugar, add the flour, and mix. in a small saucepan, bring the milk to a boil. Add a little milk to the beaten yolks and mix until the yolks are warm; add back to the rest of the hot milk and mix thoroughly. Cool the mixture rapidly. stir in the hazelnut paste. Care- fully blend the mixture with the italian meringue, and then gently stir in the unsweetened whipped cream. Pour the mixture into individual molds and freeze for at least three hours. Unmold and serve.

4 Servings

9 oz. (250 g) strawberries, hulled

1 cup (250 ml) water

3/4 cup plus 3 tbsp. (185 g) sugar

1/4 lemon, quartered

stRAwBeRRY sORBet

squeeze the juice from 1 quarter of the lemon.

Combine the strawberries with the water and sugar in a blender and puree. Add the lemon juice. Refrigerate the mixture for at least 3 hours. freeze in an ice cream maker according to the manufacturer's instructions.

Preparation: 20 minutes

freezing: 3 hours

APPle stRUDel

4 Servings

Preparation: 1 hour

Resting: 30 minutes

Cooking: 20 minutes

fOR tHe DOUGH

2 cups (250 g) all-purpose flour

2/3 cup (150 ml) water

4 tbsp. (20 ml) extra-virgin olive oil

Pinch salt

fOR tHe fillinG

1 3/4 lbs. (800 g) apples

3 1/2 oz. (100 g) raisins

3 1/2 oz. (100 g) pine nuts, or about 2/3 cup

1/2 stick (57 g) unsalted butter

2-3 1/2 oz. (57-100 g) breadcrumbs, or 1/2-1 cup

cinnamon, as needed

fOR DeCORAtinG 1 large egg

confectioners' sugar, as needed

Mix the flour with the water, oil and salt on a work surface and knead until the dough is smooth and homogeneous. form it into a ball, cover with plastic wrap, and let rest for at least 30 minutes.

Meanwhile, prepare the filling for the strudel. Peel and slice the apples. soak the raisins in a bowl of lukewarm water for 15 minutes; then drain the raisins and press to remove excess water.

Melt the butter in a large skillet. Add the apple slices, raisins, pine nuts, and a pinch cinnamon. stir in enough breadcrumbs to reach your desired filling consistency. Heat the oven to 350°f (180°C) and line a baking sheet with parchment. with the back of your hands, stretch the dough into a thin sheet on a lightly floured work surface. spoon the filling along the long side of the pastry, leaving a 2 inches (few cm) border and roll it up, making sure it is well sealed by pressing down along the edges with your fingers and curling up the two ends.

in a small bowl, lightly beat the egg with a fork. Brush the strudel with the egg. set it on the prepared baking sheet and bake for about 20 minutes. A few minutes before it is done, dust with powdered sugar and finish baking. serve with whipped cream, if you like.

Viennese CAKe

4-6 Servings

Preparation: 45 minutes

Cooking: 45 minutes

fOR tHe CAKe

3/4 cup (115 g) peeled, sweet almonds 1/10 oz (3 g) bitter almonds or apricot kernels

generous 2/3 cup (137 g) sugar

1/4 cup plus 2 tbsp. (45 g) all-purpose flour

1 1/2 tbsp. (12 g) potato starch or cornstarch 1/4 cup (25 g) unsweetened cocoa powder vanilla powder

salt

3 oz. (82 g) dark chocolate

5 tsp. (25 g) unsalted butter

5 large egg yolks

4 large egg whites

fOR tHe fillinG

4 oz. (120 g) apricot jam

tsp. (20 ml) orange liqueur

fOR tHe GlAZe 2/3 cup (170 ml) cream

tsp. (25 ml) glucose syrup

oz. (170 g) dark chocolate

Heat the oven to 350°f (180°C) and grease and flour a 9x5 inch (23x13 cm) pan. in a food processor, finely grind the almonds with 2 tbsp (25 g) of sugar. transfer to a bowl and then mix in the flour, starch, cocoa, vanilla, and a pinch of salt.

Melt the chocolate and butter together in a heatproof bowl that fits snugly over a pot of barely simmering water (or in the microwave). stir occasionally until the chocolate is melted and smooth; remove from the heat. in a bowl, beat the yolks with 4 tbsp. (50 g) of the sugar. in another bowl, beat the egg whites with 1/3 cup (62 g) of the sug- ar. lighten the beaten yolks with one-third of the beaten egg whites, then add the melted chocolate and butter. Combine the mixture with the almonds, flour, starch, and cocoa. fold in the remaining egg whites. Gently mix, using a soft spatula and stir- ring from the bottom up. Pour the mixture into a greased, floured pan.

Bake for 40 to 45 minutes. let cool completely. Remove the cake from the pan and cut the cake horizontally into three layers. Make the filling by stirring together the apricot jam and the orange liqueur in a bowl. spread the filling between the cake layers, and spread more jam over the surface of the cake. to make the glaze, chop the chocolate and put in a heatproof bowl. in a small saucepan, boil the cream with the glucose syrup and then pour over on the chocolate. stir with a wooden spoon until the mixture is smooth and velvety. frost the cake with the glaze.

tiRAMisÙ

4 Servings

Preparation: 30 minutes

Resting: 2 hours

large pasteurized egg yolks 2 large pasteurized egg whites 10 tbsp. (125 g) sugar

1 cup (250 g) mascarpone

tsp. (25 ml) brandy (optional)

1 cup (200 ml) sweetened coffee

8 savoiardi (lady fingers)

unsweetened cocoa powder, as needed

in a bowl, beat the eggs yolks with most of the sugar, heating the mixture slightly in a heatproof bowl that fits snugly over a pot of barely simmering water. in an- other bowl, whisk the egg whites with the remaining sugar.

stir the mascarpone into the egg yolks, then add the stiff egg whites and carefully fold so the mixture remains light and frothy.

Dip the lady fingers in the sweetened coffee (if you wish you can add a little brandy) and place them in the bottom of a dish (or in four small dishes or glass- es). then pour in a layer of the cream mixture and continue alternating layers of biscuits and cream. Refrigerate the tiramisù for about two hours.

Garnish with a generous sprinkling of cocoa.

4 Servings

3/4 cup plus 1 tbsp. (100 g) all-purpose flour

1/4 cup (25 g) finely ground cornmeal flour

6 tbsp. (75 g) sugar

2/3 stick (75 g) unsalted butter, softened

2 1/2 oz.(75 g) ground almonds

1 large egg yolk

1 pinch (0.5 g) baking powder

14 oz. (25 g) whole almonds

grated lemon zest, to taste

CRUMBle CAKe

Preparation: 20 minutes

Cooking: 10 minutes

in a bowl, mix all the ingredients together, except for the whole almonds. Knead to make a crumbly mixture. Put the mixture in a 7 1/2-9 1/2-inch (20-25 cm) diameter mold, pressing down lightly, and decorate with the whole almonds.

Bake in the oven at 350°f (180°C) until the crumble cake is golden, about 18 minutes.

4 Servings

4 large egg yolks

2 tbsp. (25 g) sugar

generous 3/4 cup (200 ml) Moscato d'Asti or other Muscat wine

3/4 cup plus 2 tbsp. (220 ml) heavy cream

2 sheets (1/7 oz.) gelatin

COlD ZABAGliOne witH MUsCAt wine

in a pan, preferably copper, beat the egg yolks lightly with the sugar and wine. set the pan over low heat and continue cooking until the zabaglione becomes frothy and has thickened.

Meanwhile, soak the gelatin in cold water, then squeeze out the excess water. Add the gelatin to the egg and wine mixture.

Remove the zabaglione from the heat and let cool. whip the cream and carefully fold it into the cooled zabaglione. Pour into individual bowls and refrigerate for at least 2 hours before serving.

Preparation: 15 minutes

Resting: 2 hours

Cooking: 10 minutes

CPSIA information can be obtained
at www.ICGtesting.com
Printed in the USA
BVHW090912290621
610723BV00004B/1295

9 781803 071800